Life on the Dark Side of the Cross

Supporting Depressed People

Ali Walton

Assistant Priest, Thorley, Hertfordshire

GROVE BOOKS LIMITED
RIDLEY HALL RD CAMBRIDGE CB3 9HU

Contents

The Cover Illustration is by Peter Ashton

First Impression March 2000
Reprinted June 2006
ISSN 0144-171X
ISBN 1 85174 427 4

1
Introduction

There are many experiences which can be described as 'depression': the 'Monday morning' feeling; feeling 'blue'; feeling that life consists of a bottomless pit. Some people live their daily lives with low levels of energy, whilst others suffer from such severe forms of depression that life no longer seems worth living and medical intervention is required.

> *A psychiatric nurse to a patient: 'You mustn't feel ashamed of suffering from depression. It can affect anybody.'*

Depression is no respecter of persons. It can hit anybody at any time. A spell of depression may last from a few days to weeks, months or even years. The average duration is four months, but one in eight diagnosed as suffering from depression (an illness known as 'clinical depression') is still ill after two years.

Two-thirds of the population have a significant experience of depression during their lives—that is, a form of depression which interferes with and disrupts normal daily life. At any given time one in twenty is experiencing some form of depression. It is twice as common in women as men and occurs more frequently in older people. Ten per cent of those suffering from clinical depression are referred to psychiatrists. Two per cent of sufferers are admitted to psychiatric hospitals.

These are sobering statistics. Depression is still felt to be an unmentionable problem with some degree of social stigma—and even prejudice—attached to it. Euphemisms are still used for it:

> *Has Susan recovered from her 'spot of bother'?*

> *My husband is off work suffering from 'stress.'*

> *I had a few problems a couple of years ago but I'm better now.*

> *Evelyn didn't go to church for a little while—she went through a 'dark night of the soul.'*

The imagery in my title *Life on the Dark Side of the Cross* arose when I saw a stone cross standing on a pedestal outside the Abbey Gate in St Albans, Hertfordshire. On winter nights the cross is floodlit. It looks impressive, but more striking is the dark shadow of the cross which is thrown onto the wall behind. During a time when I myself was depressed I felt I could not identify with the lit cross, but I could identify with the black shadowed cross behind it. This gave rise to my title, for it seemed to sum up where I felt I was in relation to God. My experience is not at all unusual for a Christian who is suffering from depression.

Even in our churches it is often more acceptable to talk of death and cancer than to admit to suffering from depression or some other form of mental health problem.

For these reasons it is vital for those involved in any form of pastoral care to be aware of what depression is and how to support those affected by it. This booklet is aimed at church ministers, housegroup leaders, those involved in counselling or prayer ministry, or concerned family and friends. There are no quick-fix answers to caring for those affected by depression. This booklet seeks to identify what depression is and to look at three theological models which provide frameworks for supporting those affected by it. The italicized 'cameos' throughout are based on real people's experiences as they have shared them with me, but I have created amalgams of experiences and used fictitious names.

2

'The Blues' to 'The Bottomless Pit': What is Depression?

The word 'depression' is used to refer to anything from the 'Monday morning' feeling, feeling 'blue' or low in spirits, to a severe depressive illness. To think about how to support those who are affected by depression it is important to identify what the term means.

To some, depression is a mood, to others it is a particular kind of experience. To others it may mean a particular attitude to life, and to some depression is an illness.[1]

Janet: 'I was speechless when my GP told me I was suffering from depression. I always thought of depression as sitting in the corner and crying all the time, not having headaches and no energy.'

The symptoms of depression are many and varied. They differ in type and severity from one individual to another and from mild to severe forms. Symptoms fall into four main categories, with some overlap: physical, emotional, mental and spiritual.

Physical Symptoms
Physical symptoms of depression may include:
- headaches
- aching joints
- nausea
- constipation
- a feeling of lack of co-ordination and a sense of falling over (in more severe forms)
- sleep problems—either not sleeping during the night or sleeping too much during the day

- stomach aches
- changes in appetite reflected in weight loss or gain
- blurred vision
- extreme fatigue
- loss of sexual desire
- irregularity or complete cessation of menstruation in women.
- over-sensitive hearing

Emotional Symptoms
Emotional symptoms may include:
- a lowering of mood
- loss of confidence and self-esteem
- anxiety
- loss of enjoyment of previously enjoyed activities

- feelings of worthlessness
- feelings of guilt and shame
- inability to face people
- tearfulness or wanting to cry but being unable to

---

1   R Mitchell, *Depression* (Harmondsworth: Penguin, 1975) p 7.

- feelings of isolation, unreality and an unawareness of surrounding people
- suicidal thoughts or attempts at suicide.

- loss of sense of humour
- irritability
- feelings of hopelessness

Mental Symptoms

Mental symptoms may include:
- inability to concentrate
- phobias

- forgetfulness and indecision
- a slowing of thought processes

- feelings of the brain being in separate disconnected parts with feelings of a loss of co-ordination and feelings of disorientation in time and place.

Spiritual Symptoms

For a Christian affected by depression, spiritual symptoms may include:
- a loss of awareness of God's presence or a sense of God's absence
- an inability to pray, read the Bible or go to church
- feelings of being rejected or even hated by God.

Peter didn't go to church for weeks when he was suffering from depression because he thought that he had committed the unforgivable sin, that God hated him and was punishing him.

Origins, Triggers and Causes

The origins, triggers and causes of depression are numerous and complex. It may be reactive (that is, triggered by an event external to a person) or it may be endogenous (arising from within a person for no apparent reason). It may have genetic, hereditary, economic or social causes. It may arise from physical factors— following childbirth (post-natal depression) or viral illnesses, such as 'flu, glandular fever or thyroid problems.

Personality traits may also play a part in triggering a period of depression. Perfectionists are more likely to suffer from depression. Life events such as bereavement, redundancy, divorce and retirement can be triggers. Even 'happy' events, such as marriage, having a baby or a long-awaited promotion at work may cause depression.

Another significant factor for some is lifestyle. People who work very long hours, who do not allow themselves the time to take proper meals and who do not do enough to relax and meet their social and recreational needs may leave themselves vulnerable to depression.

Julie found she had to work longer and longer hours to achieve the same amount. The harder she worked, the less time she allowed herself to spend over meals and relaxing at home. Eventually she went to her GP because she barely had the energy to get out of bed in the morning. She was signed off work suffering from depression. Her GP sent her to a counsellor who helped her to work out a more balanced lifestyle. Julie is now back at work and managing her time well. She says she now sees friends and does things outside work which she never made the time to do before.

Treatment

As Julie's example shows, treatment for depression varies. 'Talking therapy,' like the time Julie spent with a counsellor thinking about her lifestyle, is one option. Anti-depressant drugs are beneficial to many. Many who have benefited from drug therapy speak of initial resistance to it, partly due to the common myth that anti-depressant drugs are addictive, partly because of the perceived inadequacy of not being able to cope with life and partly because of the unpleasant side-effects of some drugs. Generally, side-effects are experienced before there is any apparent benefit. This leads some to stop taking anti-depressants before they begin to alleviate the symptoms.

For those whose experience of depression is severe, referral to a psychiatrist and admission to a psychiatric hospital may be appropriate. With depression which proves resistant to other forms of treatment, the drug lithium carbonate or electro-convulsive therapy may be used. ECT involves giving a light anaesthetic to relax the muscles. An electric current is then passed through the brain for a split second. This current is thought to act by stimulating electrical activity in the brain which has slowed down due to the depression. It is only used in a minority of cases where the depression is severe.

Common Mistakes in Supporting those Affected by Depression

John reports: 'Whenever anyone told me to pull myself together, to stop feeling sorry for myself, to praise God that he was with me in my darkness or that I would be a stronger Christian once I had recovered, I felt like thumping them. Most people really didn't have a clue what I was going through.'

Sadly, neither John's experience nor his reaction is at all unusual. Such insensitivity often serves simply to increase the agony and isolation of depression.

Other well-meant comments may include:

- 'Don't get so wound up and emotional.'
- 'Let's jolly you along and take you out of yourself.'
- 'All this navel-gazing is doing you no good.'
- 'It's a sin to be depressed—you should trust God more.'
- 'There must be unconfessed sin in your life which is causing this.'
- 'All depression is from Satan.'
- 'You should be praying and trusting God for healing—your faith must be weak.'

All of these, when said to someone who is suffering from depression, are likely to be prize blunders. Often they spring from ignorance about depression and the way it affects people. Sometimes, though, these comments arise from a sense of helplessness on the part of those standing by and watching someone suffer. Relatives and friends may not know what to do when they receive no response to their efforts to help. To carers in this situation any action may seem better than none. Supporting a depressed person may be prompted by the helper needing to feel in control of a situation which seems chaotic, disordered and out of control. It may feel as though the darkness engulfing and destabilizing the depressed person has come from nowhere. Caring for a depressed person may therefore be felt as a threat to the helper. After all, if it is possible for the depressed person to experience darkness apparently out of the blue, then the helper may worry that the same could happen to him or her.

One of the first things to realize in thinking about supporting those affected by depression is that it is all right to feel helpless. We are imperfect human beings. We cannot have answers to all the problems all the time. Watching others suffer will often make us feel helpless. This is just about bearable when we watch TV news about unknown people elsewhere in the world; when we watch close relatives or friends suffer, the feelings of helplessness can be unbearable.

To feel such helplessness does not mean that we are weak or inadequate. It is therefore not to be feared or covered up with inappropriate action. Not acting is better than acting in a way which, with the best intentions in the world, only increases the suffering of those we love and seek to help. How much better to admit our helplessness and look for support from people who know what help is most appropriate.

A difficult aspect of making the blunders we have identified is not what is actually said. Depressed people are already likely to be saying such things—and worse—to themselves. What *is* damaging is to hear such words coming from others, because this reinforces depressed people's negativity about themselves and increases their sense of alienation. This is why it is so important to think about how to support those who are affected by depression.

The church is not immune to such insensitivity. As people who claim to be the body of Christ on earth today, it is particularly important that congregations and individuals are aware of ways they can represent Christ to those suffering the physical, mental, emotional and spiritual anguish of depression. The rest of this booklet will consider how we may do that.

Hart's Three-stage Model

An American psychologist, Archibald Hart, has suggested that the progress of a period of depression has three phases: onset, middle and recovery. This is a helpful tool in thinking about how to support those affected by depression. Each phase has its own characteristics and needs. What may be helpful in terms of support at the onset stage may not be as helpful in the middle and recovery stages.

We shall now look at each stage in turn using a theological model which will help to identify pastoral needs at each stage, how best to meet those needs, and how to offer support to those affected by depression, whilst avoiding the blunders we identified.

3

A Model of The Shepherd in Supporting Those Affected by Depression

The Shepherd and Hart's Onset Stage

In this section we shall concentrate on Hart's onset stage and how the model of the shepherd can help us in offering support. Some people's experience of depression is a long-term lack of energy which may, or may not, spill over into clinical depression. Such people can best be seen as being at this stage.

Some people slide quickly to the point where depression becomes an illness. For others this point creeps up more slowly. A key strategy in treating depression is to identify this starting point, as it helps to identify the cause of the depression. Hart characterizes this stage as the time when the biochemical and neurological changes which occur in depression establish themselves.[2]

As some people are unaware of becoming depressed it is important that those in pastoral ministry know and recognize the signs, so that those affected can be encouraged to look for the appropriate help as soon as possible.

The shepherd has been a model for pastoral care for many years. It carries with it qualities of healing, sustaining, guiding, strong and courageous leadership, gentleness, sensitivity, and tender love and concern.[3]

From Scripture we learn much about what it means to care for others as shepherds care for their flocks. Perhaps best known is Psalm 23, which describes God as a shepherd who meets the needs of his flock, leads them along safe paths, and uses his rod and staff to guide and rescue his sheep. The shepherd may even have used his rod to treat some of the diseases that sheep suffer from.[4] Isaiah 40.11 offers a beautiful picture of the shepherd gathering lambs in his arms, carrying them and leading them gently. Isaiah's shepherd is also prepared to suffer to ensure the safety of the sheep (Isaiah 53.6). The shepherd searches for lost and stray sheep, binding up the injured and strengthening weak sheep (Ezekiel 34.16).

In the New Testament a well-known passage is John 10, where Jesus describes himself as the good shepherd who will lay down his life for his sheep. The shepherd cares so much for his sheep that he is prepared to make sacrifices to ensure their well-being. There, Jesus also affirms that he knows his sheep, that his sheep know him and will follow where he leads because they trust him.

2   A D Hart, *Coping with Depression in the Ministry and Other Helping Professions* (Dallas: Word, 1984) pp 65–70.

3   W B Oglesby, 'Shepherd/Shepherding' in R J Hunter (ed), *The Dictionary of Pastoral Care and Counselling* (Nashville: Abingdon Press, 1990) p 1164; A V Campbell, *Rediscovering Pastoral Care* (London: Darton Longman & Todd, 2nd edn, 1986) p 30; D Benner, *Psychotherapy and the Spiritual Quest: Examining the Links between Psychological and Spiritual Health* (London: Hodder & Stoughton, 1988) p 26.

4   D Tidball, *Skilful Shepherds: An Introduction to Pastoral Theology* (Leicester: IVP, 1986) p 45.

'The Shepherd' as a Model for Support

Stuart says: 'If only someone had suggested early on that I may be depressed I would have gone to the doctor then and we could all have been saved from months of pain.' The portrait of the shepherd in Scripture shows qualities which we can use in looking how to support those affected by the onset of depression.

One of the important characteristics of a shepherd is that *the shepherd knows the flock as individual sheep*. This is also true of those involved in pastoral ministry. We need to remember that:

No-one can expect to lead God's people unless the relationship is formed first. The pastor needs the intimate knowledge of his (or her) people and they need to feel confident in his (or her) leadership and able to trust that he (or she) will not lead them into any danger.[5]

Thus it is not only important for a pastor to know the important facts about each member of the congregation or housegroup, but also to know them at a deeper level, including each person's emotional and spiritual characteristics.

Where those involved in pastoral ministry know individuals as the shepherd knows the sheep, it will be clear when all is not well in an individual's life. The pastor can then make suitable enquiries and encourage the person to look for help.[6] As the cameo of Stuart (above) shows, when this happens unnecessary suffering may be limited.

To reverse this, where those in pastoral ministry do not know the members of their flock well, the onset stage of depression can be missed and the appropriate help not found until the depression is well established.

A church minister says: 'Before my wife suffered from depression I didn't know anything about it. Having suffered with her, I can now begin to look for it as a possible problem when somebody comes to me for help.'

We discovered that the Bible's pictures of the shepherd showed *someone who has some knowledge of the diseases that sheep might suffer from*. This was no mere text book knowledge—it was practical. The shepherd could spot a sheep suffering from a particular disease and then do something about it. The same should be true of the Christian pastor.

In the case of depression, those in pastoral ministry should be familiar with depression in its various disguises, from its milder to its more severe forms. It is important to be familiar with symptoms, causes and triggers.

With such information at hand, pastors will know, when meeting with a person who comes for help, whether depression is a possibility. Knowing whether the person has recently had experiences which may trigger depression, such as bereavement, will also be invaluable. As Autton writes:

If the priest is a true pastor, it is he who first observes the mentally ill (includ-

---

5   Tidball, *Skilful Shepherds* p 86.
6   F Lake, *Clinical Pastoral Care in Depression* (Clinical Theology Association, 1965) p 44.

ing those showing signs of depression), and is therefore responsible for doing something about them...Every priest should have a working knowledge of mental disorders, their diagnosis and therapy.[7] This can be a sobering responsibility. The main responsibility of the shepherd, and of the Christian pastor, is to make sure that both sheep and people do not suffer unnecessarily.

In remembering the spell of depression that Jane suffered from, she said that the most helpful thing for her was the few people who were prepared to sit with her in her darkness for however long it lasted.

We saw that *the good shepherd needs to be prepared to suffer for, and with, the sheep.* Those involved in pastoral ministry also need to be ready to suffer with those they care for.

To do this for those who are affected by depression can be very costly. Depression is characterized by burdens of enormous darkness. To a person affected by depression there is no light at the end of the tunnel—or if there is, it is seen as a train coming straight towards them! The darkness of depression can go on for days, weeks, months or years.

Effectively pastoring people who face such darkness means journeying to 'the dark side of the cross' with them—and not only journeying, but staying there with them for as long as it takes.

Some may find that they are not able to do this because entering into another's darkness causes them to come too close to their own fear and darkness. There is no shame in this. Pastors who admit this, and provide another means of support for their flock, are far less likely to cause further suffering than those pastors who ignore their own fear and darkness, become involved in supporting a depressed person and then have to withdraw because the burden is too great. When caring for a depressed person it is vital not to make a commitment to doing something and then pull out because the commitment has become unsustainable. A depressed person will interpret the breaking of a commitment as further evidence that they are worthless. It is better for a helper to be realistic from the start and only make a commitment to something that can be fulfilled.

Pastoral care in the onset stage of depression will therefore involve the pastor entering the dark places of depression as these begin to be felt by the sufferer. Listening patiently, carefully and acceptingly to the negative and pessimistic thoughts expressed by the sufferer is one way of doing this. A result is that the sufferer will feel less alone and fearful. In being a shepherd, the pastor will have achieved a great deal in meeting pastoral needs at this stage.

One of the hardest things about supporting Cliff whilst he was depressed was to keep on visiting him even when he said nothing when I was there.

---

7   N Autton, *The Pastoral Care of the Mentally Ill* (London: SPCK, 2nd edn, 1969) p 4.

This is the comment of a person trying to stay close to someone suffering from depression, and it reflects one of the functions of a shepherd: *a shepherd aims to stay close to the sheep* in order to lead and help them.

Whilst it may not seem very significant, this is something that those involved in pastoral ministry can do, which others, such as a doctor, cannot do to the same extent.

Staying close in this way is, Marion Ashton suggests, the main role for the pastor.[8] It can be achieved by regular visiting, even when the visitor is met with very little response. To begin regular visits and then to stop is likely to cause feelings of rejection on the part of the depressed person. But to stay close in this 'shepherdly' way shows depressed people that they are not alone on the road.

I felt so much better when my pastor told me that not wanting to pray or go to church were spiritual symptoms of depression, and that I wasn't to worry about it.

As we have seen from Scripture, at times *a good shepherd will actually carry the sheep*. In supporting those affected by the onset of depression, it is important that those involved in pastoral care 'carry' those they care for. It is particularly important that pastors do not add to the burdens already being carried by coming out with the blunders that we looked at in chapter 2 above.

Speaking practically, at the onset stage of depression a person is likely to go to someone who has some sort of pastoral responsibility for them and say that church services do not feel as helpful as they did, or that praying is harder work than it used to be, or that God seems much further away than in the past. At this stage, the sufferer is helped most if the pastor shows that this is all right, rather than suggesting that the person is somehow at fault in the way they express their faith.[9]

Summary

The suitability of the shepherd as a model for supporting those at the onset stage of depression is seen by looking at the qualities which the good shepherd has. Practically, pastors can use this model by:

- knowing the symptoms and triggers of depression
- knowing the people in their care and their life situations
- encouraging people to seek further help where required
- entering into the darkness that the depressed person is beginning to feel
- staying close by visiting regularly even when this meets with no response
- avoiding adding more burdens by suggesting some fault in the person's faith.

8   M Ashton, 'Depression' (Tape of talk at London Institute of Contemporary Christianity, April 1985).
9   F Lake, *Clinical Theology: A Theological and Psychological Basis to Clinical Pastoral Care* (London: Darton Longman & Todd, abridged edn, 1986) pp 85–86.

4
The Body of Christ as a Model for Pastoral Care in the Middle Stage of Depression

Hart's Middle Stage

Hart's second stage in depression is characterized by the greatest misery. The depressed person feels that there is no end to it. Uncharacteristic behaviour and personality changes will be noticeable. The sense of isolation and alienation cause depressed people to withdraw from others into their own world. They may need other people to do things for them that they would normally do for themselves.

Patrick says of this stage: 'I dreaded everything: getting up, because I knew I faced another interminable day of exhaustion and misery; going to bed, because I knew that I would lie awake for hours. I couldn't face anyone, do anything or see any end to it. I tried to pray but God just was not there. He seemed to ignore all my cries for help. I just wanted to be left alone to die.'

It is at this stage anti-depressant drugs can be extremely valuable in treating the symptoms of depression and in providing a way for the depressed person to bear their pain. Pain, in all its shapes and forms, is the major feature of depression in this stage. Whilst the depression may have been triggered by any number of life issues this is not the stage to engage in counselling or therapy to deal with these. The depressed person is likely to be too debilitated to make use of these 'talking' therapies. At this stage, basic survival is the name of the game.

Patricia comments: 'When I was depressed I appreciated the vicar from church coming to see me every week, but what I also needed was somebody to do my ironing.'

Patricia says something very important. It is good for pastors to keep visiting someone who is depressed. It is also important to understand that others in a church can play a vital part in caring for depressed people. Ross writes:

> The challenge of caring for depressed people is daunting, but one we are all called to do if we are to 'Carry each other's burden' (Galatians 6.2).[10]

Caring for depressed people is not the sole responsibility of those who work full-time for the church. It may be that the care offered to depressed people is impoverished if only those who work for a church in a formal way are involved, because of the many pressures they face. It is something a whole church congregation can share. In this sense each person may be a pastor, because each is a small part of a larger unit which the New Testament refers to as 'the body of Christ.'

---

10   A Ross, *Helping the Depressed* (Eastbourne: Kingsway, 1990) p 67.

The Body of Christ in Scripture

Paul uses the picture of the body to describe the Christian church (Romans 12.4–5). Just as we each have a body made up of many parts, each having their unique function, a church congregation is also like a body. Individual members of a church body have their own functions and the sum of all the individuals makes the whole.

Paul uses the same picture in 1 Corinthians 12.12–27 to say that the individual members of the body are dependent on each other. If even one small part is missing, or not working properly, the body is not complete. If one part of the body suffers, the rest suffer with it.

'The community of all believers' is an important resource which is often overlooked.[11]

If many members of a church are involved in caring for others, then the burden of caring for depressed people may be spread around.

Mary felt guilty about her support of a depressed person. She was the only one doing it. Eventually, she had to offer less support because she got very tired. She said, 'If only there had been more of us involved from the start I could have carried on longer.'

It is difficult for pastors to be all things to all people. Because of the incidence of depression in the population there are likely to be people in a church who have been depressed in the past. They may be able to offer support and understanding in ways which take pressure off the pastor. Their experience can be used by God to help others. Expressing the idea of caring and community like this is central to being the body of Christ.

One of the great strengths in using the body of Christ as a model for pastoral care is that it means that everybody can be involved. It does not require a theology degree, a counselling qualification or a position of leadership in a church. It simply involves the desire to care for others in ways which are appropriate for each situation. This may mean that the pastor visits weekly or that a housebound person steps in to pray, whilst other parents help with trips to and from school, and practically-minded people help with household or gardening jobs.

The Body of Christ as a Model for Pastoral Care in the Middle Stage

The body of Christ can work in several ways as a model for caring for depressed people. One way involves members of the body in a particular place doing things *for* the person. Another way involves doing things *on behalf* of the person. Some ways of caring may involve both of these.

---

11   R W Fairchild, 'Sadness and Depression' in Hunter (ed), *Dictionary of Pastoral Care and Counselling* p 1105.

Praying for the Depressed Person

Hart's description of this middle stage suggests that a depressed person may need others to do things for them that they would normally do for themselves. For a Christian who is depressed, this may include praying on their behalf.

Patrick's story continues: 'I felt guilty because I wanted to pray as normal, but I couldn't. I worried about this a lot until my doctor, who was also a Christian, said that it was my turn to allow others to pray for me. It was such a relief when I heard this.'

Being unable to pray is one of the spiritual symptoms for a depressed Christian. It does not mean that something has gone disastrously wrong in their relationship with God. If something was wrong, their inability to pray would not cause them pain. One way of caring is to give reassurance about this, as Patrick's doctor did. It is an extremely distressing feeling. A depressed Christian needs to be reassured without being patronized.

Another way of caring is to provide assurance that other members of the body will be praying for the person. Actually praying with a Christian who is depressed is something that should only be done with the person's permission. If the offer to pray is declined, they should not be made to feel guilty about it.

Offering to pray for the things and people that the depressed person would normally pray for is also helpful. Praying on the behalf of a depressed Christian may also help to minimize feelings of guilt about not being able to pray. Having been depressed himself, John Young writes:

At such times, we rightly depend upon the faith and prayers of other believers to support and sustain us.[12]

Joining in Holy Communion

At services of Holy Communion the body of Christ remembers that Jesus gave his life for his people. At one point in the Anglican service the congregation says, 'We are one body, because we all share in the one bread.'[13]

Depressed people may be cautious about attending communion services. They may be afraid of crying during the service because their feelings of worthlessness may make them feel unworthy of joining in. They may fear the greater intimacy of a communion service. The prospect of close contact with others during the service, such as at the Peace, may fill them with terror. The sense of intimacy with God expressed through the service may be too much for them to bear at a time when they feel abandoned by God. They will know whether or not they can cope with these things and their reticence should be respected. At the same time they should be reassured that, however real their feelings of worthlessness may seem, they are not outside God's love. They should be reassured that the time will come when they once more feel able to receive the bread and wine.

---

12   J Young, 'In the Valley of the Shadow of Death' *Church Times* 9 June 1995 p 5.
13   *The Alternative Service Book* (London: SPCK, 1980) p 142.

Barbara says: 'When I was in the psychiatric unit the chaplain used to visit me every week. Every week he asked me if I wanted him to bring me communion. Every week I said no. I was impressed and reassured because he did not make me feel bad about this and he still kept coming to see me.'

Continuing to receive communion should be encouraged because of its thera-peutic value. It emphasizes the grace of God at work in his people. It is the place where our felt worthlessness meets God's love—and we re-learn how much we are worth to him. It reinforces the fact that the depressed person is still a member of the body of Christ, however isolated and alienated he or she may feel. It is here that both God and the Christian community can 'carry' and care for the depressed. It also allows the mystery of God's work to be active in the person's life. The bread and wine of the communion service may be seen as 'God's medicine': something which is powerful and active to be taken alongside medication prescribed by doctors. Many Christians who have been depressed speak of the power of this 'medicine' even though they cannot tie down how it worked.

Bearing One Another's Burdens

Galatians 6.2 encourages us to carry one another's burdens. The body of Christ is vital to this. Depressed people may feel so weighed down that they badly need to feel that they are not alone. Having someone else providing a sense of sharing the burden is important.

This may be costly for someone who is staying close to a depressed person. It may be days, weeks, months or even years before the person is able to respond to this sense of closeness. In the meantime, it is tempting for the carer to give up. Doing something costly but not receiving a response is discouraging. It requires patience, perseverance and self-sacrifice from the carer.

Jean says: 'One of my friends who lives in another town was depressed. I phoned her every week for months. She didn't say anything much in all that time. It was like carrying on a monologue. Sometimes, I didn't want to ring because of this. But I kept phoning and now she's better she says those phone calls were like a lifeline to her.'

If Jean had been the only one supporting this friend it would have been very hard for her to keep going. Fortunately she knew her friend's church were also being very supportive and so she knew she was not carrying the burden on her own. In this case the body of Christ worked well in supporting Jean's friend.

The Church as a Form of 'Therapy'

Ross believes that the church needs to:

…regain the ability seen in Jesus to spot and care for the needy individual in the crowd (Mark 5.26; Luke 19.2–10). At its best the church can be a therapeu-tic community that restores and repairs those in need through its worship, ministry and people.[14]

This idea has been taken further by Hudnutt, who suggests that the body of Christ is a form of 'therapy.' He believes that it involves caring for people in a way that allows them to express their darkest thoughts and most negative emotions.[15]

Churches tend to be places where people feel they have to put on their 'happy faces.' If asked how things are many Christians will smile and say, 'Fine, thank you,' even if they are struggling with life. Depressed Christians feel this pressure even more because of an unspoken attitude in many churches that Christians do not get depressed. This attitude makes depressed Christians feel even more isolated and alienated. They simply cannot put on a happy face and pretend everything is fine. Many end up not going to church at all whilst they are ill.

Churches where people feel free to be open about their negative emotions and dark thoughts can be places of healing for all, particularly the depressed.

Sylvia was an assistant minister in a church when she was signed off work suffering from depression. Although it was scary, she decided to be vulnerable and tell the congregation the truth about her illness. After that a significant number of people went to her and told her either that they had been depressed in the past or that they were currently depressed. Sylvia's honesty gave permission for people in that church to admit to their struggles. It then became a 'therapeutic' church in which people found healing and support.

Care, Acceptance and Support

Part of being a 'therapeutic' church is caring, accepting and supporting members unconditionally. The body of Christ should provide a warm, loving, understanding and compassionate atmosphere of friendship and acceptance. Winter believes that this is one of the greatest needs of depressed Christians:

They often feel they are a burden to everyone and that others will be impatient with their weakness. God's gracious acceptance of us, not for what we achieve but just for who we are, should ideally be mirrored in our acceptance of each other.[16]

Carrie says how important this was to her: 'When I was depressed I still went to church. But I didn't have the energy to wash my hair, iron my clothes or wear clothes which matched. I was always late because it took me so long to get out of bed and get there. When I was there I just cried through the whole service. Some people looked at me as though I was making the place dirty and shouldn't be there. But most people accepted me as I was, spoke to me, brought me coffee and made sure I had something to eat. I will never forget these people because of the way they loved and accepted me. It felt like they were caring for me as Jesus would.'

---

14 A Ross, *Helping the Depressed* p 70.
15 R K Hudnutt, *Meeting God in the Darkness* (Ventura, California: Regal Books, 1989) p 51.
16 R Winter, *The Roots of Sorrow: Reflections on Depression and Hope* Basingstoke: Marshalls, 1985) p 280.

Graciousness in the Face of Doubt

Christians who are depressed will doubt their faith. This is one of the spiritual symptoms of the illness. They may doubt that God loves them. They may even wonder whether God exists at all. It is profoundly unhelpful if others criticize them. This is where it is important for the body of Christ to act on behalf of the depressed person. Depressed Christians should be reassured that their doubts are a symptom and will pass. Until that time they need to know that other members of the body of Christ will hold onto their faith for them and will continue to believe in their recovery. As a depressed Christian recovers, their faith begins to function again and they will no longer need the faith of others to give theirs shape.

Summary

The importance of the body of Christ as a model for pastoral care in the middle phase of depression should not be underestimated. Because each member of the body has a different gift and part to play no-one should be excluded from caring for depressed people.

Practical ways to live this out might include:

- making sure that care and support is practical and offered in a reassuring way. The depressed person is not yet ready to receive a lot of hopeful words or meaning-making phrases;
- practical tasks such as offering lifts, doing the ironing, shopping, gardening or other odd jobs, picking children up from school, and so on;
- the pastor visiting regularly;
- people praying *for* the depressed person *and on their behalf;*
- staying close to the person providing constant reminders that they will get better and that their faith will function again and that they are not completely alone;
- gently encouraging the person to keep going to church and receiving the bread and wine at communion;
- loving and accepting the person however untidy, dirty and dishevelled they may look;
- making them feel wanted and welcome at church services however late they may be, or however distressed they may be during the service.

5
The Cross of Christ as a Model for Pastoral Care in the Recovery Phase of Depression

We shall now be looking at the cross of Christ and how it provides a model in caring for those in Hart's 'recovery' phase of depression.

Carrie says: 'When I was depressed I really wanted to find some meaning in it. It all seemed so pointless. It was only as I was beginning to get better that I could begin to see that Jesus did understand what I was feeling because he went through much worse.'

Hart's Recovery Phase

The transition from the middle phase to the recovery phase of depression is not usually marked by anything dramatic. However, one sign may be that the depressed person begins to ask questions about the meaning of this experience: why it did it have to happen? Why did God abandon me when I needed him most? The hint of life in a person's voice, a slight care about appearance, a glimpse of laughter—all these may be indicators that recovery is beginning. The carer needs to be vigilant in spotting these hints, and protecting them as a gardener protects tender shoots in springtime.

Hart suggests that during this phase the sufferer will begin to have moments of feeling better. These may occur at unexpected times. They may bring some relief to the sufferer. However, they may also make the person feel worse when their mood drops slightly.

The road up out of depression is not an even one. It does not have a gradual and steady incline. It tends to be a series of mountain peaks and valley bottoms. Overall, the peaks get higher and the dips are not as deep. However, to the one who is recovering, the valley bottoms will make more of an impression than the mountain tops. A dip down into a valley may be interpreted as a sign that the depression is recurring again in full force. Those in a supporting role need to prepare the sufferer to expect these peaks and valleys. There needs to be a lot of encouragement and reassurance that the valley bottoms really are getting less deep and the mountain peaks are lasting longer.

Jean says: 'I thought I was never going to get better, but one day I realized I had felt less miserable for a few hours. Gradually, those hours got longer and became whole days. I got so disappointed, though, when I had a bad day after several good ones. I can see now that I was getting better, but it couldn't be measured in days. It was a slow process with lots of ups and downs on the way. I wish someone had warned me that it would be like this.'

The Theology of the Cross of Christ

The cross of Christ provides a good model for pastoral care in the recovery phase, because it touches the issues that people face when they are coming out of a period of depression. Generally they meet two main problems: one is how to make sense of the feelings of having been abandoned by God, felt earlier in the depression. The other is the need to find some point or meaning in the suffering.

Isaiah's suffering servant (Isaiah 53; 61.1ff) speaks clearly to someone who has been depressed. Luke 4.16ff shows Jesus identifying himself with the suffering servant. So what is said of the suffering servant can be said of Jesus.

Lake uses these thoughts when he asks what God has to do to reach someone who is depressed. He believes that it is:

...only by (Jesus) himself accepting their lot, and inflicting upon himself their affliction. He must overcome the infinite distance they have had to place between themselves and any would-be rescuer. He must taste death for every man. He must make his own bed in hell. This, to his eternal glory by Christ Jesus, he has done.[17]

Psalms such as 22, 69 and 88 are known as *psalms of dereliction*. These also show the effectiveness of Christ's work on the cross. *Christ's cry of dereliction* from the cross shows that he experienced feeling abandoned by God. He quotes Psalm 22.1 and cries, 'My God, my God, why have you forsaken me?' This means that there is actually an experience in Jesus' life which depressed people can look to when they feel God has abandoned them. They are not alone in their sense of abandonment. Being able to identify with Jesus in this helps depressed Christians to feel less alone.

Patrick says: 'I tried to pray when I was depressed but all I seemed able to say was, "My God, my God, why have you forsaken me?" because I felt God had completely abandoned me. I felt so alone and such a failure. It was only when I remembered that Jesus himself said this on the cross that I felt better about it.'

1 Peter 3.18–19 shows that after he died, Jesus descended to the dead and preached to the spirits in prison for three days before his resurrection. This is commonly interpreted to mean that *Jesus spent three days in hell* after his death.[18] It is possible to understand 'hell' as a place of isolation and rejection.[19] If so, then Jesus certainly knew what it was like to feel isolated and rejected.

It can be said that through the suffering of Jesus, *God suffers with humanity*.[20] Jürgen Moltmann's work *The Crucified God* offers one basis for saying this. It is the suffering of Jesus that somehow makes it possible for people to feel less alone and to make sense of their own suffering.

17   Lake, *Clinical Theology* p 67.
18   R T France, 'Exegesis in Practice: Two Samples' in I H Marshall (ed), *New Testament Interpretation* (Exeter: Paternoster Press, 1977); W Grudem, *1 Peter*, Tyndale NT Commentaries (Leicester: IVP, 1988) p 204.
19   A Canale, *Beyond Depression: A Practical Guide for Healing and Despair* (Rockport: Element, 1992) p 125.
20   F Bridger and D Atkinson, *Counselling in Context: Developing a Theological Framework* (London: HarperCollins, 1994) p 180.

The Cross of Christ as a Model for Pastoral Care in the Recovery Phase

It is clear that the cross of Christ speaks to those recovering from depression in a host of different ways. Because it is so important we need to understand more about it.

One of the many pastoral needs depressed Christians have is to discover a sense of hope in Christ, that the depression will end *and that the suffering is not meaningless*. One of the signs of recovery is that a sense of hope gradually begins to spring up where previously there has been overwhelming hopelessness. As Winter shows, such hope can be found in Christ:

This is the perspective which gives hope: we are being changed. There is purpose in it all. God does bring good out of the apparent chaos of this fallen world. In us the image of God is being restored right now. This is the mystery, which is Christ in you, the hope of glory. Without Christ in us, there would be no hope in this world or beyond.[21]

Carrie says: 'When I was depressed I couldn't see any meaning in it. I used to hate those people who reminded me that God uses everything for the good of those who love him. If he loved me, why was he making me suffer like this? I couldn't see any meaning in it or any hope that it would end. A while after I was better someone told me they were depressed. I told them some of the things that had helped me. They said it was the most helpful conversation they'd had since they started to be ill. All of a sudden I realized I couldn't have done that if I hadn't been depressed. I realized that God was using me and my experience to help someone else. Suddenly it felt as if it did have some meaning after all. That short conversation changed my view of my illness and my view of God.'

The feelings of *desolation and abandonment* are two of the most powerful feelings experienced during a time of depression. Christians are often taught that God is there to meet every need and he is present in every situation of our lives. A Christian suffering from depression has probably been used to praying and asking God for help in difficult situations. Yet in one of the hardest experiences of all, God is marked by his absence. He does not seem to answer the depressed person's cry for help. He does not seem to offer his strength as a resource. At the time of blackest despair when a person needs God most, he seems to be silent and powerless.

Even when someone is fully recovered from other symptoms of depression, these feelings of abandonment and isolation can continue to leave people lost and cut off from their faith.

Jean says: 'Even when I was better, I still found it hard to pray and trust God because I felt he had let me down when I needed him most.'

---

21 Winter, *Roots of Sorrow* p 302.

People involved in caring for those recovering from depression need to know that, at this point, the sense of identifying with Jesus' own experience of abandonment on the cross can be the most powerful resource that can be offered. Winter writes powerfully:

> In deepest depression we can remember that he [Jesus] cried out from the cross, 'My God, my God, why have you forsaken me?' So when we walk through the valley of the shadow of depression and even death we know that he has been that way before us.[22]

During recovery, one thing that people need is the sense of their experience being transformed. *The power of transformation in the cross* should not be underestimated. This need for God to transform the sense of suffering can be found in the power of the cross of Christ. Lake states:

> It is the direct activity of God in the gospel of Christ which alone has power to transform a person trapped in depressive dynamics into one who is rooted and grounded in the life of the Son of God.[23]

As well as a sense of transformation, people recovering from depression also need to have *feelings of connection* restored to them. The sense of isolation, alienation and desolation experienced during depression cause the sufferer to feel disconnected from themselves, from others and from God. The recovery phase is the time when the desire and need to feel reconnected surfaces.

Patrick explains: 'When I was depressed I felt disconnected from God and unable to hold on to him. A friend gave me a wooden cross, called a "holding cross" which I could hold in the palm of my hand. It was something solid and tangible which helped me to feel that maybe there was still a connection between me and God.'

This sense of re-connection with God, which Patrick found through physically holding a cross, fulfils a great pastoral need. Others may find pictures or icons helpful. Some may find music to be a way forward. It does not matter how this sense of re-connection with God through the cross of Christ happens. What does matter is that those supporting people recovering from depression listen carefully to them in order to discover with them a way for this to be experienced.

One of the things that depressed people need when they are recovering is the feeling that *there is new life* springing up in them. Often the help of someone else is needed to encourage and nurture this. It must be remembered that the greatest promise of all concerning new life can be found in the death of Christ on the cross and his resurrection. It is a mystery that something as horrific as the crucifixion of Christ can lead to new life, but it is a mystery to be rejoiced over. It is a mystery that is particularly relevant to the pastoral needs of a Christian who is recovering from depression. It is at this time that the help of trained professionals can be most valuable. Full-time members of a church's staff, spiritual directors, counsel-

---

22 Winter, *Roots of Sorrow* p 304.
23 Lake, *Clinical Theology* p 76.

lors and therapists may all have a part to play as the person tries to make sense of their experience in order to move on from it.

Summary

We have seen that the cross of Christ is an important model for identifying the pastoral needs of people recovering from depression. It involves supporters, carers and pastors in using the model to speak gently and sensitively to the one recovering to help them resolve faith issues that remain with them after their experience of depression. These faith issues are likely to include:

- why wasn't God there for me when I needed him most?
- why did he leave me feeling so cut off from him, so desolate and so abandoned by him?
- why did God seem powerless to change the situation?
- why did God leave me feeling so hopeless for so long?
- how can such an awful experience have any meaning?
- how can I know more of the new life that others seem to have?

These are all questions which Christians recovering from depression are likely to ask (though it is not an exhaustive list!). It is important that those caring for them, supporting them and pastoring them have a sufficient understanding of Christ's work through his death and resurrection that they are able to answer these questions. Trying to answer such questions will best meet the pastoral needs of the person in recovery.

6
Conclusion

We have looked briefly at what depression is and have seen that it seems to have three phases. We have seen how caring for people suffering from depression can be helped by the use of three models, one for each phase: the shepherd, the body of Christ, and the cross of Christ. For each of these models I have suggested practical ways that pastoral care can be exercised.

It is worth noting that the model of the cross of Christ could be developed further, to become a model in its own right for meeting pastoral needs at each stage of depression. For instance, the onset phase could be seen through the eyes of Jesus praying in the Garden of Gethsamene shortly before his arrest, where he asked God the take the cup of suffering from him (Matthew 16.36–46; Mark 14.32–42; Luke 22.39–46). As a person becomes aware of the increasing pain of descending into depression, their major desire is for that suffering to be lifted from them.

Pastoral needs in the middle phase can be characterized by Jesus' experience of suffering abandonment, isolation and rejection during his crucifixion (Matthew 27.32–56; Mark15.21–41; Luke 23.26–49). In the middle phase of depression, Jesus' sense of abandonment by God speaks into the experience of the depressed person feeling themselves abandoned by God.

In the recovery phase, Jesus' resurrection to new life after his death speaks to the pastoral needs of the depressed. As the blackness of the depression begins to lift, the person feels a sense of new life which identifies with Jesus' own experience.

Our final note needs to come from 2 Corinthians 1.3–4:

> Praise be to the God and Father of our Lord Jesus Christ, the Father of compassion and the God of all comfort, who comforts us in all our troubles, so that we can comfort those in any trouble with the comfort we ourselves have received from God.

This principle has been alluded to several times during this booklet. It is important to recognize that all that we experience in life can have the redemptive function of which Paul speaks in these verses. Suffering from depression does not fall outside this principle of redemption. Those who have suffered from it may have found it meaningless at the time. However, those who have experienced it are in a far better place to help those currently suffering from its scourge than those who have never experienced it. This is not meant to put a 'spiritual' gloss over it. It is actually something profound that we all need to grasp. Even those experiences in life that seem pointless and which we would rather not have, can be used by God, through his redemptive purposes, to help others. In this way, experiences which seem pointless and meaningless can actually become the most profound experiences of our lives. As we think of caring for depressed people, this is a principle which we need to keep in our minds.